# THE HISTORY OF MEDIEVAL INDIA

## DAKSH WADHWANI

This book is dedicated, with great reluctance, to my Parents, Rajesh and Swati, because they forced me to do it.

# Contents



**The End Of Medieval India**

# Foreword

This Book is purely expressing information about The Medieval Of India , written and composed by Daksh Wadhwani. It contains very much indformation about the different periods of India Medieval and you will be able to gain information in a good manner of words.

# Preface

Medieval India refers to a long period of the history of the Indian subcontinent between the "ancient period" and "modern period". It is usually regarded as running between the breakup of the Gupta Empire in the $6^{th}$ century AD and the start of the Mughal Empire in 1526, although some historians regard it as both starting and finishing later than these points.

# Acknowledgements

This book is written by Daksh Wadhwani, a student , academist and a novelist.He is a very profound reader and a good reader who loves to gain a lot of information whenever he gets an oppurtunity in every place.

*Prologue*

## Medieval Indian History

Medieval India is the phase of the Indian subcontinent between the ancient period and the modern period. This phase can be related to the time period between the $6^{th}$ century and $16^{th}$ century.

# 1

# Early medieval period

The start of the period is typically taken to be the slow collapse of the Gupta Empire from about 480 to 550,[11] ending the "classical" period, as well as "ancient India",[12] although both these terms may be used for periods with widely different dates, especially in specialized fields such as the history of art or religion.[13] Another alternative for the preceding period is "Early Historical" stretching "from the sixth century BC to the sixth century AD", according to Romila Thapar.[14]

At least in northern India, there was no larger state until the Delhi Sultanate, or certainly the Mughal Empire,[15] but there were several different dynasties ruling large areas for long periods, as well as many other dynasties ruling smaller areas, often paying some form of tribute to larger states. John Keay puts the typical number of dynasties within the subcontinent at any one time at between 20 and 40,[16] not including local rajas.

Pratihara dynasty, was the last largest dynasty of northern India which rivaled the Gupta empire in extent and ruled most part of India from 6th century up-to 11th century. They can be differentiated from other kingdoms as they were called Imperial Pratiharas.

- Chalukya dynasty ruled most of the western Deccan and some of South India, between the 6th to 12th centuries. Kannada-speaking, with capital at Badami.
- Rashtrakuta dynasty, was a Kannada Dynasty ruling large parts of the Indian subcontinent between the 6th and the 10th centuries and one who built World Heritage center Ellora, Maharashtra.
- Eastern Chalukyas, 7th and 12th centuries, a South Indian Kannada-Telugu dynasty whose kingdom was located in the present-day Andhra Pradesh they were the descendants of Western Chalukyas.
- Pallava dynasty, rulers of Telugu and some Tamil areas from the 6th to 9th centuries.
- Pala Empire, the last major Buddhist rulers, from the 8th to 12th centuries in Bengal. Briefly controlled most of north India in the 9th century.
- Chola Empire, a South Indian empire which ruled from Tamil Nadu and extended to include South-east Asian territories at its height. From 9th century to 13th century.
- Empire of Harsha, a brief period of control of most of north India, from 601 to 647, under Harsha of the Vardhana dynasty.
- Western Chalukya Empire, ruled most of the western Deccan and some of South India, between the 10th to 12th centuries. Kannada-speaking, with capital at Badami.
- Kalachuri dynasty, ruled areas in Central India during 10th-12th centuries.
- Western Ganga dynasty, was an important ruling dynasty of ancient Karnataka, often under the overlordship of larger states, from about 350 to 1000 AD. The large monolithic Bahubali of Shravanabelagola was

built during their rule.

- Eastern Ganga dynasty, was a royal dynasty ruling Odisha region who are descendants of Kannada Western Ganga Dynasty and Tamil Chola Empire. They have built famous Konark Sun Temple and Jagannath Temple, Puri.
- Hoysala Empire, a prominent South Indian Kannadiga empire that ruled most of the modern day state of Karnataka between the 10th and the 14th centuries. The capital of the Hoysalas was initially located at Belur but was later moved to Halebidu.
- Kakatiya Kingdom, a Telugu dynasty that ruled most of current day Andhra Pradesh, India from 1083 to 1323 CE.
- The Sena dynasty, was a Hindu dynasty that ruled from Bengal through the 11th and 12th centuries. The empire at its peak covered much of the north-eastern region of the Indian subcontinent. The rulers of the Sena Dynasty traced their origin to the south Indian region of Karnataka.
- Kamarupa, 4th to 12th century in Assam, ruled by three dynasties.

# 2
# Late medieval era

—♡—

The Late Middle Ages or Late Medieval Period was the period of European history lasting from AD 1250 to 1500. The Late Middle Ages followed the High Middle Ages and preceded the onset of the early modern period (and in much of Europe, the Renaissance).[1]

Around 1300, centuries of prosperity and growth in Europe came to a halt. A series of famines and plagues, including the Great Famine of 1315–1317 and the Black Death, reduced the population to around half of what it had been before the calamities.[2] Along with depopulation came social unrest and endemic warfare. France and England experienced serious peasant uprisings, such as the Jacquerie and the Peasants' Revolt, as well as over a century of intermittent conflict, the Hundred Years' War. To add to the many problems of the period, the unity of the Catholic Church was temporarily shattered by the Western Schism. Collectively, those events are sometimes called the Crisis of the Late Middle Ages.[3]

Despite the crises, the 14th century was also a time of great progress in the arts and sciences. Following a renewed interest in ancient Greek and Roman texts that took root in the High Middle Ages, the Italian Renaissance began. The absorption of Latin texts had started before the Renaissance of the 12th century through contact with Arabs during the Crusades, but the availability of important Greek texts accelerated with the Capture of Constantinople by the Ottoman Turks, when many Byzantine scholars had to seek refuge in the West, particularly Italy.[4]

Combined with this influx of classical ideas was the invention of printing, which facilitated dissemination of the printed word and democratized learning. Those two things would later lead to the Protestant Reformation. Toward the end of the period, the Age of Discovery began. The expansion of the Ottoman Empire cut off trading possibilities with the East. Europeans were forced to seek new trading routes, leading to the Spanish expedition under Christopher Columbus to the Americas in 1492 and Vasco da Gama's voyage to Africa and India in 1498. Their discoveries strengthened the economy and power of European nations.

The changes brought about by these developments have led many scholars to view this period as the end of the Middle Ages and the beginning of modern history and of early modern Europe. However, the division is somewhat artificial, since ancient learning was never entirely absent from European society[citation needed]. As a result, there was developmental continuity between the ancient age (via classical antiquity) and the modern age[citation needed]. Some historians, particularly in Italy, prefer not to speak of the Late Middle Ages at all but rather see the high period of the Middle Ages transitioning to the Renaissance and the modern era.

# 3
# Historical Overview of Medieval India

## Northern India

### The Gupta aftermath

The early $6^{th}$ century saw the rapid decline of the Gupta empire, its powers weakened by devastating raids by the Huns from central Asia. By c. 565, when the Hun attacks had waned, Gupta power had vanished. Northern India was covered by numerous independent kingdoms.

### Harsha Vardhana

In the first half of the $7^{th}$ century, these kingdoms were forced to submit to a single ruler. This was the warrior-emperor Harsha Vardhana (ruled 606-647). Launching a series of campaigns from his capital, Kanauj, he brought the whole of northern India under his control.

At Harsha's death his empire at once fell apart, as the vassal rulers asserted their independence. Again northern India was divided into numerous kingdoms.

### The Arab invasion

In the early 8th century, the westernmost regions of the Indian subcontinent were occupied by Arab armies.

The Arabs had burst out of their Arabian homeland in the 7th century, impelled by their new faith, Islam. They had conquered Iraq, Iran, Syria, Egypt and North Africa, and now invaded Spain, in the west, and India, in the east. The regions of Multan and Sindh became provinces of the new Arab empire, the mighty Islamic Caliphate.

These conquests had a permanent impact on the subcontinent. Over time the populations here were converted to Islam, and the territories covered by Multan and Sindh form the heartlands of today's Pakistan.

**The struggle for Kanauj**

The kingdom of the Gurjara-Pratiharas stood in the way of further Arab encroachments into India, and Gurjara victories over the invaders brought them to prominence. At the end of the 8th century and in the early 9th century they expanded their power to control Kanauj and dominate northern India, with the exception of the wealthy Pala kingdom in the east.

The city of Kanauj, Harsha's former capital, retained a certain aura of imperial glory about it, and to possess it was to lay claim to supremacy over the whole of northern India. The ruler who controlled Kanauj could expect numerous lesser kings in the region to offer their submission.

The Gurjara-Prahitas were not left in undisputed overlordship for long. Their position was contested by the Pala dynasty of Bengal. This dynasty is notable for being the last major Buddhist dynasty in India. It maintained strong religious and diplomatic ties with the Buddhist states of South East Asia, and under them the great university of Nalanda reached the peak of its influence.

The Pala themselves could not establish an enduring preeminence in north India either. Indeed, over the next two centuries three kingdoms fought for control of Kanauj and regional supremacy: the Gurjara-Pratiharas, based in the northwest; the Palas, in the northeast; and another kingdom based further south, in the Deccan, that of the Rashtrakutas.

The history of northern India throughout the 9th and 10th centuries was dominated by the wars between these three powerful states. All three held Kanauj at some time or other, but never for long. The main theater of warfare lay in an area located in the heart of northern India, called the "Kanauj Triangle"; and the period is known in Indian history as the "Tripartite Struggle".

One outcome of this near-continuous warfare was the rise to prominence of a warrior aristocracy called the Rajputs. Members of this group would establish several dynasties in the next period of India's history.

By the end of the 10th century, the situation was changing. The Rashtrakuta dynasty collapsed in 973, by which time Gurjara power was also on the wane. The Pala kingdom lasted for another two hundred years, but was never again able to assert dominance in the region – indeed, for much of that time it was fighting for its life.

## Central India

In the Deccan plateau of central India, the kingdom of the Chalukya dynasty dominated from the 6th through to the mid-8th century, when it was replaced by the Rashtrakutas. In the late 10th century their power declined and the Deccan became fragmented amongst a host of smaller states. The most important of these were the

Western Chalukya, Hoysala and Kakatiya kingdoms.

## Southern India

By 500 CE southern India was dominated by three rival kingdoms, the Cheras, Pandyas and Cholas. In the early 7th century, the Pallavas rose to preeminence, and dominated southern India until the late 9th century. The Pandyas were then briefly the strongest power in the south, and the Cholas then dominated south India from the early 10th century through to the early 13th century.

The peoples of southern India were active in the maritime trade of the Indian Ocean, and this led the rulers of all the states just mentioned to try and project their power overseas. Their main target was Sri Lanka, but their efforts met with little success until the 11th century, when the Cho succeeded in establishing their rule over the northern part of the island. The Chola also even projected their power as far as South East Asia.

## Islamic expansion into Medieval India

The first major incursion of Islam into the Indian subcontinent had occurred in the 8th century, as we have seen, when Arab armies occupied Multan and Sindh.

In the 9th century the Muslim rulers of Sind and Multan became effectively independent from the Caliphs in Baghdad, and they and their successors seem to have given up any further ambitions of territorial expansion.

## Mahmud of Ghazna

The rise of aggressive new Muslim powers in central Asia changed this.

At the very end of the 10$^{th}$ century, a fearsome Turkish leader, Mahmud of Ghazna, began launching a succession of devastating raids deep into India. They ranged deep into the Ganges plain, and wrought immense destruction on well-known Hindu centers – specially targeted by the Muslim raiders. They sacked the city of Kanauj and destroyed Gurjara power.

These campaigns showed how disunited India had become, fragmented amongst numerous small kingdoms and principalities. Although many states in the north-west were now ruled by warrior-princes called Rajputs, they failed to coordinate their efforts and could be picked off one by one.

## The Delhi Sultanate

Unsurprisingly, other Muslim leaders from central Asia decided to take advantage of this situation, and at the end of the 12$^{th}$ century one of them, Muhammed of Gur, began a systematic conquest of the subcontinent.

Muhammed's armies soon occupied a large part of northern India. These armies were commanded by slave generals, and on Muhammed's death one of them asserted his independence and, with the city of Delhi as his capital, took the title of sultan.

Albeit with many set-backs, the sultanate of Delhi gradually extended its power so that by the mid-14$^{th}$ century it had subjugated all but the southernmost region of the subcontinent. Almost immediately, however, the sultanate went into precipitous decline. A great rebellion snatched the southern half of the empire from its control, and this huge region came to be divided between two powerful states, the Muslim sultanate of Bahmani, and, in the far south, the powerful Hindu kingdom of Vijayanagara.

The sultanate of Delhi continued its decline so that by the mid-15<sup>th</sup> century its territories included only the city of Delhi itself and some area around it

## Many sultanates

The receding frontiers of the sultanate left in their train a hotchpotch of states. In the northern half of the subcontinent, apart from a group of Rajput kingdoms which had never really been incorporated into the Delhi sultanate's territory, these were all ruled by Muslim sultans. The Delhi sultanate may have declined, but it had left a legacy of Muslim control throughout much of India. The next great empire in India's history would be able to build on that. This was the Mughal empire.

# 4

# Religious Developments in Medieval India

Medieval India saw the triumph of Hinduism over both Jainism and Buddhism. Jainism became very much a minority religion, while Buddhism all but died out in the land of its birth.

Buddhism was still widespread in the Gupta empire, at the end of the ancient era. Its spread throughout India had been due to its appeal as a faith which, much more so than the ancient Vedic religion, answered people's yearning for a more personal connection to the divine.

## Hinduism on the ascendant

Even by Gupta times, however, the challenge of Hinduism was growing. Evolving from the ancient, but still deeply revered, Vedic beliefs and practices, Hinduism had incorporated many features of Buddhism. Popular cults such as Vaishnavism (the worship of Vishnu) and Shaivism (the worship of Vishnu), which had grown up in the centuries before 500 CE, were much more devotional than the ancient Vedic religion had been. At the same time they were deeply rooted in ancient Vedic beliefs, in a way that Buddhism was not. They thus had a deep appeal for the population at large.

Hinduism also strengthened by it adoption of the monastic practices of Buddhism. Large Hindu monastic communities grew up which became places of advanced study, fostering the intellectual development of Hindu culture.

## Buddhism on the decline

In medieval India, this reinvigorated Hinduism increasingly crowded out Buddhism, both as a popular religion and as an intellectually satisfactory system of belief. It became an increasingly defined faith, with clearer lines of demarkations viz-a-viz Buddhism. Indian medieval rulers now found themselves having the choose: whereas in ancient times kings were often patrons of Vedic, Buddhist and Jain establishments, in medieval times this was less possible. Most increasingly opted for Hinduism, and by the $9^{th}$ century the only significant Buddhist rulers in India were the Pala kings in the northeast. Within the borders of their realm, as we have noted, was located the great Buddhist university of Nalanda, which must have bolstered the Pala kings in retaining their loyalty to their ancestral (but by-now minority) faith.

When northern India came under fierce attack from Muslim armies based in central Asia, from the beginning of the $11^{th}$ century, Indian populations found themselves challenged by the forces of an alien and hostile religion. This must have created a need for them to unite behind the banner of an indigenous faith of their own. The only possible candidate for this was now Hinduism.

This factor must have hastened the decline of Buddhism, and it is certainly the case that this great faith largely died out in India some time in the following centuries. A decisive moment in this process must have been the sack of the great Buddhist university of Nalanda in about 1200 CE, and the fall of the Pala dynasty at about the same time.

# 5
# Society and Economy in Medieval India

The increasing dominance of Hinduism in the religious sphere had significant impacts on Indian society. Although the new Hinduism was very different from the ancient Vedic religion in many ways, it regarded itself as the heir and guardian of Vedic teachings.

## Caste

Most importantly, the rise of Hinduism went hand in hand with a rise in the status and authority of the Brahmin priestly caste. These were now widely regarded as the religious experts par excellence.

Unsurprisingly, given their place at the top of the caste hierarchy, the Brahmins promoted caste divisions. This development was already apparent under the Gupta empire, by the end of the ancient period, and throughout the medieval period the caste system became more all-pervading as Hinduism spread, and more rigid.

It also became more elaborate. Hereditary occupation groups evolved into sub-castes, outside of which marriage was increasingly frowned on.

## The Status of Women

The status of women varied over time and within regions in medieval India, but the general trend was for their position in society at large, and within the family, to decline. Records show some high-status women, especially queens, being involved in government, and some participated in the fine arts, especially in the development of music and dance. Many temple dancers were well educated, and accomplished in the arts.

On the other hand, urban and rural women seem to have become increasingly restricted in their daily lives. Widows in particular suffered a loss of status, Amongst high caste women the practice of sati, the voluntary immolation of widows on their husbands' funeral pyres, first recorded from the Gupta period, became widespread during these centuries.

## Trade and Towns

International trade, both across the Indian Ocean and up into central Asia, brought many foreigners to medieval India, such as Arabs, Persians, Chinese and people from the Malay Peninsula. Persian Zoroastrians fleeing persecution from Muslims in Iran came to India and formed the Parsee colonies there. Christian groups established themselves in ports on the southwest coast of the subcontinent. Jewish communities had existed in towns and cities across India since ancient times.

Large Muslim trading communities also grew up in the ports of India. In fact, in the medieval period Muslim merchants and sailors took over more and more of the Indian Ocean trade, becoming the dominant group. This was aided by developments within India itself. As Hinduism spread and Brahmin teachings become more prominent, maritime trade became increasingly frowned on for devout Hindus. It polluted them by bringing them into close contact with foreigners, who were outcastes and therefore ritually unclean.

The Indian Ocean trade nevertheless increased in medieval times, and this naturally boosted trade within the subcontinent. New trading towns emerged. Shravanabelagola, in south India, for example, developed from a religious settlement in the 7$^{th}$ century to being an important commercial centre in the 12$^{th}$.

Other towns flourished as pilgrimage centers, which also brought trade. Whereas in ancient India Hindu temples had been small affairs, with small shrines set in walled enclosures and with much of the public worship conducted in the open air, in medieval India huge temples rivaled the wealthy Buddhist monasteries of earlier times.

Large temples supported by royal patronage served religious, social, and judiciary purposes. Temple building served a commercial as well as a religious purpose. Merchants financed the construction of the temples to compete with the royal temples, and shrines built by rich landlords in rural areas acted as centers of authority and trade, as well as serving the religious needs of agrarian communities. Large temples of course also provided employment to hundreds of people of various guilds and professions.

# 6
# Cultural developments in Medieval India

## Language and literature

Medieval India saw the rise of regional languages as mediums for great literature. Whereas Sanskrit had been the Brahminical language of ancient India, now the Tamil dialects of South India, for example Kannada, became prominent vehicles for intellectual expression. The fact that the new Hindu cults used local languages for their sacred texts was a major part of their appeal, but even at court these regional languages replaced Sanskrit.

Nevertheless, Sanskrit retained its status as the primary language of high culture. Just as in Guptas times, works which had intellectual pretensions, or wanted to be read right across the subcontinent, were written in Sanskrit.

Literary works included poetry, grammar, lexicons, manuals, rhetoric, commentaries on older works, prose fiction and drama. They were written on palm leaves tied together into codices, or book-like forms.

Leading poets were major figures at the course of Indian rulers. Some noblemen, ministers, ascetics and monks also contributed to the literary output of the period. Poetry came in different forms, including shatpadi, six-line verses; ragale, lyrical compositions in blank verse; and ttripadi, three-line verses. The traditional champu, composed of prose and verse, also continued in use. These were sung to the accompaniment of a musical instrument.

Inscriptions on stone and copper plates were also common. These were written mostly in regional languages but some were in Sanskrit, or were bilingual. The sections of bilingual inscriptions stating the title, genealogy and origin myths of the King were generally done in Sanskrit.

Local languages were used in everyday administration and commerce, including contracts, information on land ownership, and so on.

## Architecture and Art

The kings of medieval India are famous for their patronage of art and architecture. The brisk temple building of the period is evident throughout the subcontinent, but more especially in central and southern India.

Independent architectural traditions arose in different parts of India. One of the most notable can be seen in Hoysala temple architecture of southern India. It is characterized by an attention to exquisite detail and skilled craftsmanship, reflected also in its temple sculpture, with its sensuous depictions of feminine beauty. The outer walls of many Hindu temples contained an intricate array of stone sculptures and friezes depicting the great Hindu epics.

# The End of Medieval India

After a brief revival, the Delhi sultanate was finally finished off when the last of its rulers was killed by the forces of another invader from central Asia at the battle of Panipat (1526). The victor of Panipat, Babur, went on the found the Mughal dynasty.

Another chapter in India's long history had opened. This was not just due to the rise of a new imperial dynasty, but also to the fact that influences from outside the subcontinent began to make themselves felt, moving India into the modern era. The use of firearms was an example, but more than this was the appearance of European traders along the coasts of India. From small beginnings these would come to have control over the entire subcontinent.

www.ingramcontent.com/pod-product-compliance
Lightning Source LLC
Chambersburg PA
CBHW070206160726

47997CB00017B/1525